# WALKS WITH CHILDREN
# IN THE
# LAKE DISTRICT

## KESWICK
## AND THE NEWLANDS VALLEY

Other QUESTA Guides


Walks with Children in the Lake District:
*Buttermere and the Vale of Lorton*
*Borrowdale*
*Patterdale*
*Around Coniston*
*Ambleside and Grasmere*


Walks with Children in the Surrey Hills


Walks with Children in the Yorkshire Dales:
*Swaledale and Wensleydale*
*Wharfedale*


Kielder Country Walks

# WALKS with CHILDREN
## in the Lake District
## KESWICK & THE NEWLANDS VALLEY

## Ron Bickerton

A Questa Guide

© Ron Bickerton 1998
ISBN 1 898808 02 3

Questa Publishing
PO Box 192, WORCESTER, WR2 6YH

**Also by Ron Bickerton**

Walks with Children in the Lake District:
*Buttermere and the Vale of Lorton*
*Around Coniston*

Printed by
Carnmor Print and Design,
95/97 London Road, Preston

# CONTENTS

# INTRODUCTION

*"The first thing I remember as an event
in my life was being taken by my nurse to the
brow of Friar's Crag on Derwentwater".*

Keswick's setting among the hills seems to have inspired many English poets and writers. John Ruskin, who penned the above lines, first visited the town as so many young children have, on family holidays. His connections with Keswick were to continue throughout his life, even his regrettable marriage to Effie Gray in 1848 started with a week's honeymoon in Keswick.

1871 saw Ruskin settled in the Lake District at Brantwood House, Coniston Water. Even this purchase linked Ruskin with Keswick, for it was from one of the town's home-grown writers, Eliza Lynn, that he purchased Brantwood. Born in 1822 at Crosthwaite Vicarage, Eliza's mother died within a few months of her birth and the child, the youngest of twelve children, was made the scapegoat for the mischief of her older brothers and sisters.

As she grew older Eliza became absorbed in books, teaching herself several languages and also started to write. Her decision to become a writer was encouraged by a poem being accepted by Ainsworth Miscellany. She moved to London, after many objections by her father, to become the first woman ever to write for a national newspaper.

In March 1858 her marriage to William Linton, artist and engraver, marked her return north to live at Brantwood, which was later sold to Ruskin when the marriage failed. Returning to Keswick on many occasions she was to admit that it was only the climate that prevented her from returning to Keswick permanently. After her death, in July 1898, her ashes were buried at the foot of her father's grave in Crosthwaite churchyard.

Coleridge moved into Greta Hall in July 1800, so as to be near his friend Wordsworth, now living at Dove Cottage, Grasmere. Born a few miles away at Cockermouth, Wordsworth would have passed through Keswick many times as a child on his way to school at Hawkshead. In 1803 Sir George Beaumont, an admirer of Wordsworth presented him with a small estate at Applethwaite, known as The Ghyll. Wordsworth turned the gift down, but Beaumont insisted, since it was to allow him to be near his friend Coleridge.

Knowing Coleridge would not remain at Greta for long, Wordsworth never moved to the estate. In fact it was only a few years later after an unsettled marriage that Coleridge encouraged his brother-in-law, Robert Southey, to move to Greta Hall. Southey's arrival at Greta was only to be until the wounds had healed after the sudden death of his daughter, Margaret when only a year old.

Soon the fells were to attract him and after his first ascent of Skiddaw he wrote, "Bitter bleak, next door to heaven". Contrary to his expectations, Southey was to remain at Greta for the rest of his life.

Keswick and Newlands, however, have not always been the land to inspire the poets. In 1564, Queen Elizabeth I, granted Daniel Hechstetter permission to search and dig for minerals in the area. The creation of the Mines Royal Company in 1568, saw a major growth in the town as a German miners were brought in to work the mines and increase production. Today, almost 400 years later, the mining scars have almost gone, and with first the railway and later the motor car, Keswick became a centre for people to explore the surrounding fells.

# WALK 1

# FRIAR'S CRAG, WALLA CRAG AND CASTLEHEAD

*This fine circuit of lakeshore paths, crags and woodland is an excellent introduction to the delights of country walking. During the summer you have the option of starting this walk by using the Derwentwater launch service to the landing stage at Barrow Bay.*

**Start/Finish:** Car park, near NT information centre, at Keswick boatlandings. GR265229.
**Total distance:** 10km (6¼ miles).
**Height gain:** 360m (1180feet).
**Difficulty:** Moderate, but the ascent can prove tiring on a warm day.

## THE WALK

Leaving the car park, turn left to walk past the launch piers to Friar's Crag. Then retrace your steps a few m/yds, and turn right past the monument to John Ruskin, then along the lakeshore to enter a small woodland. Keep with the path as it bends right to a gated track. Turn right, on a track past Stable Hills, to a permissive lakeshore path around Calfclose Bay to the landing stage at Barrow Bay. Cross the road and ascend the Watendlath Road to Ashness Bridge.

*Ashness Bridge an ancient packhorse bridge, and with the numerous upland paths it is evident that in days gone by there was considerable coming and going across the Borrowdale Fells.*

Don't cross the bridge, but ascend the grassy path on the left bank of the beck, cross a stile and then continue for 100m/yds to turn left and ascend to a ladder stile over a wall. Cross the stile and accompany the path round the head of Cat Gill, to a wall near the summit of Walla Crag. Cross a stile to reach the summit cairn now clearly seen.

The views across Derwentwater even on a poor day are magnificent, the Grasmoor and

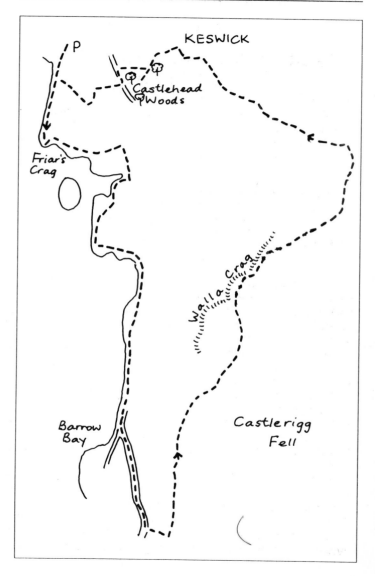

Grisedale Fells form a back-drop to the distinctive ridge of Cat Bells.

## THE WAY BACK

Leave the summit on a footpath heading north, near the edge of the crag. Pass through the wall at a gate and descend, keeping the wall on your left, to cross Brockle Beck at Rakefoot.

Follow the road for 200m/yds and then turn left on a footpath (signposted: Keswick, Great Wood). Recross Brockle Beck, turn right, keeping the beck on your right, and pass a second bridge, to reach a farm. Go through the farmyard to Spring Road and continue for 400m/yds, to take a signposted footpath left to Castlehead. At the woodland go left, then right to a fence corner, here ascend left to the summit of Castlehead.

The rocky summit has a view indicator to help you identify the surrounding fells, towns and villages. Benches also provide the excuse for a breather while enjoying the view. From Castlehead retrace your steps 200m/yds to the fence corner. Turn left and descend, through a woodland of birch, beech and oak to Borrowdale Road. Cross road to an enclosed footpath and head left for 50m/yds to a signposted path on the right. Take the path to Cockshot Wood where a path will take you left or right to the launch piers. At the pier turn right to retrace your steps to the car park.

## ALONG THE WAY
### Friar's Crag

*Friar's Crag is widely regarded as one of the most outstanding viewpoints in the Lake District, by some, the finest. At water level in the rocks below Friar's Crag can be seen a number of slate tablets inscribed with a date and initials, these tablets mark the low water level of the lake during that year, a tradition first started by Jonathan Otley in the dry summer of 1826. Otley was born near Grasmere in 1766 and came to Keswick in 1791 where he remained for the 65 years earning his living as a clock repairer. He was also renowned as a geologist and meteorologist, and lived for many years in King's Head Yard near the Moot Hall.*

*Having a close affinity with John Ruskin, a monument close by bears the inscription to his memory.*

*MDCCCXIX-MDCCCC*
*The first thing which I remember as an event in my life was*

being taken by my nurse to the brow of Friar's Crag on Derwentwater.

John Ruskin was born in London in 1819, the son of a wine merchant. He travelled widely with his parents, visiting Keswick on several occasions. He became a prodigious author, a renowned art critic, essayist, poet and philanthropist. At the age of 52 he bought Brantwood by Coniston Water, where he lived until he died in 1900.

Ruskin is buried in the churchyard at Coniston.

## Canon Rawnsley

On the way to Friar's Crag you pass a memorial tablet to Canon Rawnsley, for 34 years vicar of Great Crosthwaite, near Keswick. He was a most industrious man, and instrumental in 1902 in securing the publication of Beatrix Potter's first book, The Tale of Peter Rabbit. His most notable achievement was the foundation of the National Trust in 1895 with Octavia Hill and Robert Hunter. Rawnsley was Honorary Secretary of the National Trust from its inception until his death in 1920. Appropriately Friar's Crag, Lord's Island and part of Great Wood were given to the Trust in his memory in 1922.

## Lady's Rake

One of the many tales that abound in Borrowdale is that of Lady's Rake on Walla Crag. The story goes that in 1715 the last Lady of Derwentwater was confined to her home on Lord's Island, following her husband's imprisonment for his support of the Stuart uprising. She escaped with the family jewels, eluding her captors by climbing Lady's Rake, a steep gully on Walla Crag, hoping to obtain her husband's release. Sadly her efforts were to no avail, her husband was executed in the Tower of London for high treason. Shortly after his death there was a great display of Aurora Borealis in the night skies, and this colourful phenomenon became known as "Lord Derwentwater's Lights".

# WALK 2
## LATRIGG via THE OLD RAILWAY

*Latrigg though overshadowed by its mighty neighbour of Skiddaw, stands overlooking the town of Keswick, with views west across the town to Derwent Water and south to over High Rigg to the Helvellyn ridge, which must be among the finest in north Lakeland. By using a right of way along the disused railway, this walk follows the River Greta, recrossing it many times before making a gradual ascent to Latrigg's summit from the east. Returning to Keswick by Spooney Green Lane a popular route from the town to Skiddaw.*

**Start/Finish:** Platform of disused railway station behind Keswick Spar.
GR272238.
**Total distance:** 9km (5½ miles).
**Height gain:** 240m (787feet).
**Difficulty:** Moderate, this walk on well maintained tracks and paths presents no route finding problems.

### THE WALK

Heading east leave the platform join the trackbed of the old railway to cross high above the River Greta, keep with the track looking down on the gardens of Keswick. Passing under a road bridge press on for 400m/yds to double gates below the Greta flyover. Through the gates, turn right and ascend to the road. Immediately bear left to descend on a tree lined path to rejoin the railway above a weir on the river. Continue for 2km/1.2miles along the track, past the station platform of Low Briery and recrossing the river three time until you arrive at a stone shelter, just before a fourth bridge. Take the gate opposite the shelter, cross the field a gate leading to a lane and turn left. Accompany the lane as it bends right and ascend to a road junction. At the junction turn left, then right over a stile to a gated track (signposted: Skiddaw Underscar). Accompany the track for 850m/yds to a gate alongside a pine woodland. Through the gate, bear left and climbing to meet a parallel path which is followed along the sky-

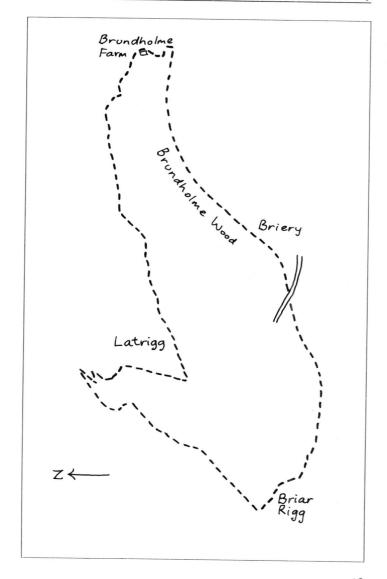

line passing through a gate to the summit of Latrigg.

## THE WAY BACK

Your return to Keswick starts by heading in a westerly direction form the summit until you arrive at a seat over looking Derwent Water. Turn right (north) on a path for 500m/yds and descend to meet a track at a plantation. Turn left and descend by the track for 1.5 km/1 mile to join Spooney Green Lane crossing the A66 to the junction at Briery Road. Cross the road to the footpath opposite and turn left, at the end of the footpath recross the road to a footpath running behind the hedge. Continue over a cross road to steps leading to the road at a round about. Here cross the road to the car park entrance at the rear of Keswick Spar and the station.

## ALONG THE WAY
### Railway and station
*Built in 1864, both the railway which linked Penrith with the west coast at Workington, and the station saw an increasing growth of visitors to the Lake District. The height in passenger traffic came in 1939 when ten trains a day called at the station. By 1961 this had declined to six and in 1966 with the increasing popularity of the motor car, the line and station finally closed. The one time sidings and track in front of the platform now serve as a car park to the Keswick Spar next door, while the station, which now stands boarded and awaiting a new role has in the past been used as a restaurant and tea room.*

### Low Briery
*Now a caravan park, the site has for more than six centuries seen many industrial uses. During the 19th century weirs where built on the river to supply power to bobbin mills. In the early years the mills used wood from local woodlands, but as trade increased the railway was used to bring in the wood as the mills produced bobbins for use in the textile industry world-wide.*

# WALK 3
## BARF and LORD'S SEAT

*Enclosed by Forestry Commission plantation the fells to the west of Bassenthwaite offer splendid walking on fine grassy ridges. This energetic walk, popular with the Victorians for the spectacular views, starts with a steep climb through the forest. The hard work is rewarded by wild flowers in spring, while in autumn the fellside is awash with wild bilberries and the purple-blue hue of heather. On a clear day once above the tree line the views are extensive.*

**Start/Finish:** Powterhow car park, near the Swan Hotel, Thornthwaite. GR 220265.
**Total distance:** 7.5km (4½ miles).
**Height gain:** 492m (1613feet).
**Difficulty:** In spite of the considerable height gain, this is a pleasant walk on well maintained paths and forest trails with a small rock outcrop to scramble.

### THE WALK

From the car park entrance cross the road, head left along the lane opposite, to a wicket gate on the right. Through the gate take a green path among the trees, passing the Clerk (white painted stone), high above on the scree stands the white painted rock known as the Bishop.

By stepping stones across Beckstones Gill, follow a waymarked path over a stile into woodland. At path junction turn right, and keep with the path to scramble over a small rock outcrop, then by zigzags to meet a forest trail. Turn right, and when the trail starts to climb, bear right to cross a fence by a step stile. Recross Beckstones Gill, and then by a steeply rising path continue to the summit of Barf.

*The summit of Barf offers remarkable views of Bassenthwaite Lake and the Skiddaw massif. Westward little is yet to be seen except for Lord's Seat and the connecting ridge.*

Heading west from Barf, make along the ridge, then by a short pull to the summit of Lord's Seat,

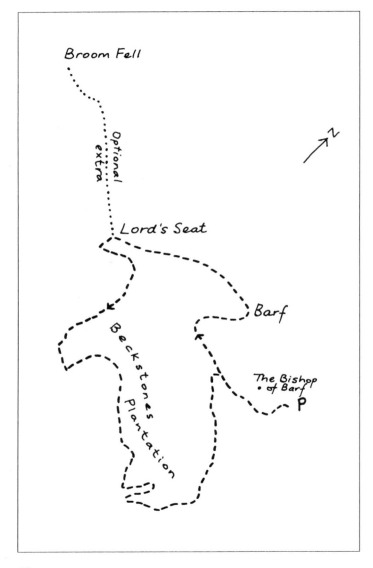

marked by a small cairn and
two iron fence stanchions.

## OPTIONAL EXTRA
By easy walking north-west
along the splendid grassy ridge
of Todd Fell, lies Broom Fell
marked by a massive cairn. This
extra walk which adds about
2.3km (1½ miles) to the overall
distance, gives excellent views
of Whinlatter and the Grasmoor
hills. Retrace your steps to
Lord's Seat.

## THE WAY BACK
You can of course, retrace your
steps from Barf, but do take
care descending the rock outcrop. A more interesting return
over Seat How and forest trails,
however, starts by descending
south to a stile. Follow the path
over boggy ground to the second path on right. Turn right
and keep with the path for 200m/
yds to join a forest trail. Shortly
after passing a group of Scots
pine look for an indistinct path
on the left opposite a vehicle
turning area. After climbing the
bank a well-trodden path
through heather and over
wooden board walks leads you
to the summit of Seat How. The
continuing path descends
steeply to a forest trail. Turning
left, then right, descend to the
next junction and turn left.

Follow this trail to a junction
with the path used on the ascent. From this trail you will have
splendid views of the Bishop of
Barf.

Turn right, and retrace your
steps to the car park.

## ALONG THE WAY
### The Bishop of Barf
*The Bishop of Barf dates from a
time when the Swan Hotel at
Thornthwaite, stood at the end
of a road and needed to attract
some of the many tourists to the
area.*

*Starting as the Monk, the
obelisk of rock was later white-
washed and the legend of
the Bishop of Barf was born.
Indeed, there is a bishop asso-
ciated with this spot, a man of
reckless habits, who was killed
trying to ride his horse up the
fell in order to win a bet.*

# WALK 4
## DERWENT WATER:
## AROUND THE LAKE

*This circuit of Derwent Water, although the longest walk in this book, is one of the finest low level walks in the Lake District. Walking in a clockwise direction gives you splendid views into the Jaws of Borrowdale and of the surrounding fells. Young children may find the distance a little too much. But, by making use of the summer launch service from one of the landing stages round the lake, you can return to Keswick, and spread the walk over two or more days. Timetables are available from any National Park Information Centre, and are displayed at each of the piers.*

**Start/Finish:** The Moot Hall, Keswick. GR266234.
**Total distance:** 15km (9½ miles).
**Height gain:** Nominal, but many undulations.
**Difficulty:** An easy but long walk that may be tiring for the very young.
Plenty of lakeside spots for breaks.

## THE WALK

Leave Moot Hall along Lake Road, past the bank. Turn right at the garage, to a subway (signposted; The Lake). Continue past the launch piers towards Friar's Crag, and at a junction bear left to a gate and the shore. The way is now clear through another gate into woodland, keep with a good path to a gate. Turn right along the access road leading to Stable Hills. Cross the cattle grid to a signposted shore path left to Calf Close Bay, with Lord's Island, and Rampsholme Island to the right. Cross Cat Gill and keep with the shore past Ashness Gate Pier.

NOTE: From Cat Gill to Ashness Gate Pier, if after heavy rain the shore path is flooded, it will be necessary to take to the footpath alongside the main road. Care should be taken as this road is very busy in the summer months.

Cross a stile to a shore path

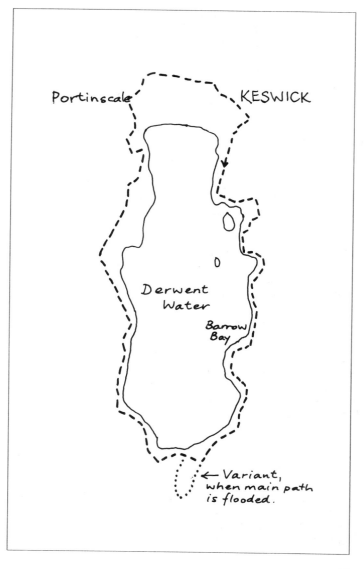

which you accompany around the headland, meeting the road again at Kettlewell car park. At the car park entrance cross the road to path behind a wall in Strutta Wood. Follow the path, right, to rejoin road shortly before Lodore Swiss Hotel. 150m/yds past the hotel take path right (signposted: Manesty) to a gated bridge across the River Derwent.

## OPTION

After prolonged rain you may find the path to Manesty, becomes flooded. If this is the case, continue along the road for half a mile to a signposted footpath on the right, about 100m/yds past the Borrowdale Hotel.

Take the path, beside a beck, to a stile. Over the stile bear right to a stile in a field corner, cross it and follow the river to the bridge.

*As you walk beside the river to your right is Shepherds Crag a favourite haunt of rock climbers, who are to be seen most days like colourful spiders on the rock face.*

This option will add 1km (3/4 mile) to your day, but will save very wet feet or a forced return to Keswick.

## TO CONTINUE

Cross the bridge, where sections of boardwalk lead to a gate in a wall in the middle of Manesty Wood. Follow the path near the shore to a cottage (The Warren), and there turn right, along a driveway to a gate at Brandelhow. Go between the buildings and bear right around a headland to High Brandelhow Pier. A pathway through agreeable woodland now takes you to a gate at Low Brandelhow Pier.

From here head left alongside a wall to a gate, and by an obvious path and a driveway go past Hawes End to a gated path (signposted: Portinscale, Keswick). Follow a clear path running between fences through woodland and open fields to cross the driveway to Lingholm (gate here).

Cross the driveway and continue with a wall to your right, past Fawe Park and on to Nichol End Marina. On reaching the marina turn left along the lane to the road, and then turn right to follow the road for a little under half a mile, until the road bends sharp left. Go right, down past hotels and across a suspension bridge spanning the River Derwent. Follow the road for 150m/yds , then by a path across two fields. On reaching the River Greta turn left, and at the road turn right to cross the bridge and follow the road to the town centre.

### ALONG THE WAY
#### Moot Hall and Keswick Market Square

*The town's market charter dates from 1276, and in the late 1770s Keswick was still a popular market selling all types of grain. There was also a custom known a hiring day, when local farm servants and labourers would parade for engagement by prospective employers, but by 1870 this custom, like many throughout northern England, had died out.*

*The building commonly known as Moot Hall stands overlooking the market square. The present building was con-*

*structed in 1812 on the site of an earlier building dating from 1517. Now housing the tourist information centre, the building has many interesting features which include a one handed clock on the tower, and a bell dated "H.D. 1001 R.O.". The date is more likely 1601, the "R.O." probably stands for Robert Oldfield, a bell-maker in the early 1600s, when this type of bell was made. I have been unable to find any record of what the initials H.D. stand for.*

#### Brandelhow

*Brandelhow was the first acquisition by the National Trust in the Lake District. The estate of 108 acres on the slopes of Cat Bells came on the market in 1902 for £6500. A public appeal raised £7500 in five months from donations large and small.*

### THE GREAT FREEZE

*During the winter of 1895, the country was in the grip of what became known as 'The Great Freeze'; skaters were seen on Derwent Water, along with photographers and vendors selling hot drinks and soup.*

*A dramatic peak was reached when, on the 6th February, thin powdery snow started to fall. Within hours it was a full blizzard driven by easterly winds lasting several days. When at last the slow thaw set in, the cracking of the great sheets of ice could be heard for miles around.*

# WALK 5
## LONSCALE FELL

*Lonscale Fell is reserved for walkers looking for peace and solitude
on those long sunny summer days. Most walkers found hereabouts
are bound, lemming like, for the long unrelenting pull to the summit
of Skiddaw. Seldom visited by walkers Lonscale Fell provides an
opportunity to tramp over grassy trackless fells, and boasts extensive
views from the Caldbeck Hills in the north, across our return route
through Glenderaterra to Blencathra and on southward to the
Helvellyn massif.*

**Start/Finish:** Latrigg car park, GR281253.
**Total distance:** 10km (6 miles).
**Height gain:** 480m (1575feet).
**Difficulty:** In spite of the considerable height gain, this is a pleasant
walk on grassy fell paths. The descent from Lonscale Fell to Burnt
Horse is very steep and care should be taken that young children do not
slip. Not recommended in poor visibility.

## THE WALK

Cross the stile at the head of the car park and turn left on a fenced path (signposted: Skiddaw, Mosedale, Bassenthwaite). After the second gate keep left alongside a fence to a small monument to the memory of the Hawells, shepherds noted for their skill in breeding Herdwick sheep.

Continue on a steep path, cross a stile, and then at wall corner turn right leaving the main trod to Skiddaw. After 20m/yds leave the fence on a clear grassy path to a small iron gate. Through the gate turn right, now with the fence on your right, and continue to a crossfence. Take the gate on the right, turn left and make for the modest cairn on the summit of Lonscale Fell.

A short walk north-east, crossing the intervening fence by a stile, will take you to the east summit with dramatic views into Glenderaterra at your feet. Do take care of children at this point; don't let them run on ahead, the drop is very sudden!

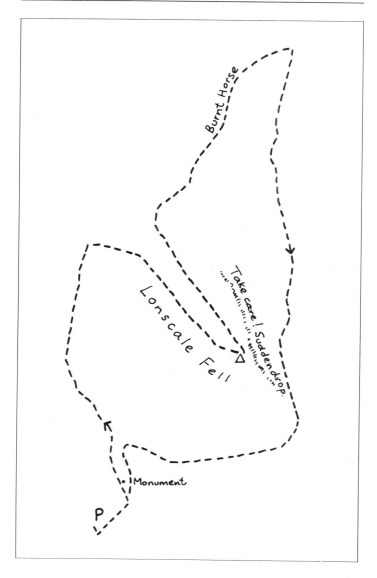

## THE WAY BACK

Leave the cairn heading north-west, first on a grassy path, then on a clear trod heading for a fence. At the fence turn right and descend to the col with Burnt Horse. Care is needed as this descent is steep and in wet conditions very slippery.

From the col follow the line of an old wall over the summit of Burnt Horse, then descend to meet a path near a wooden gate. Head south (right) on the path for 400m/yds to then accompany a wall for a further 400m/yds to a junction. At the junction take the path on the right (signposted: Keswick). Cross a wooden bridge, turn left then right on a path which contours high above Glenderaterra Beck, and below Lonscale Crags.

Shortly after passing Lonscale Crags cross a stile, then follow a broad bracken-lined track to ford Whit Beck. Leave the beck climbing steeply to the gate near the monument at the start of the walk. Through the gate accompany the wall as you retrace your steps to the car park.

---

## THE NATIONAL TRUST

*The acorn from which the National Trust has grown started with the desire of Canon Hardwicke Rawnsley, vicar of Crosthwaite in Keswick to preserve places of natural beauty and historic interest. He achieved his ambition in 1895, when, together with Octavia Hill and Sir Robert Hunter, the National Trust was founded.*
*In 1902 the Trust was to purchase its first property in the Lake District, Brandlehow Woods, on the shoes of Derwent Water, after a public appeal raised the purchase price of £6500 in only five months. today in the Lake District the Trust owns or holds on lease 16,184 hectares of land, almost all of the central fell area. Six of the main lakes, along with much of their shorelines are also protected.*
*Over 40 major footpath rebuilding projects have been undertaken in the past twelve years, along with many smaller projects on footpaths in the area.*

# WALK 6
## THE MINES OF NEWLANDS

*From Goldscope Mine on the valley floor to a mine high on Dalehead
Crags below the summit of Dalehead, this walk visits many small
entrances to mines hidden in the fellside. Dalehead Tarn nesting high
among the hills makes a ideal spot to rest and reflect how life must
have been during the heyday of the mines. There is much of fascination
on this walk, but all children must be closely supervised and kept well
away from mine shafts.*

**Start/Finish:** Chapel Bridge, Little Town. GR 221194.
**Total distance:** 10km (6 miles).
**Height gain:** 530m (1740feet).
**Difficulty:** Moderate; most of this walk is on well-made tracks and
grassy, miners' paths. Care is required in the vicinity of mine openings
as many have shafts hundreds of feet deep.

### THE WALK

Set off on the road crossing
Newlands Beck to a gated track
on your left to Newlands Church.
At the church bear left on a
track to Low Snab, (Sign on
gate: No public right of way permission of landowner. Keep to
farm track). Cross the farmyard
to a gate below the waste heaps
of Gold Scope Mine.

Keep to a wall on the left and
follow it to a wooden bridge to
recross Newlands Beck. A clear
grassy path takes you to a stone
track. Turning right, the way now
continues past a climbing hut to
the dressing floor and waste

heaps of Castlenook Mine.

From the mine path descend
to ford the beck. Take a rising
green trod left, past a small mine
entrance. Cross Far Tongue
Beck to the remains of a stone
hut (Dale Crag Mine). Leave
the hut on a steeply climbing
path among boulders and
heather to a cairn standing on a
flat plateau.

Just above is the entrance to
Dale Crag Mine, the highest
mine in Newlands. Keep well
away from this entrance as the
surround is very loose and the
hole over 300 feet deep.

A contouring path across the

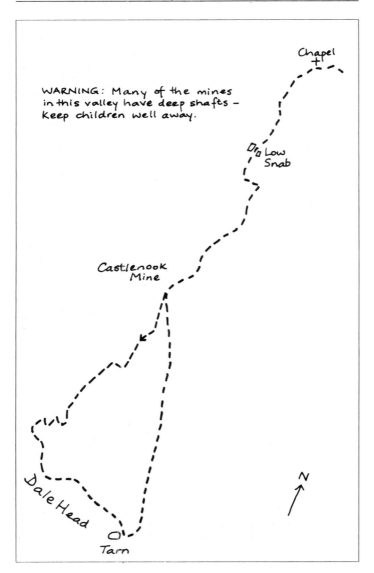

WARNING: Many of the mines in this valley have deep shafts – keep children well away.

Chapel

Low Snab

Castlenook Mine

Dale Head

Tarn

N

scree takes you to a grassy shoulder marked by a cairn. From here descend by stone steps to Dale Head Tarn.

At this point you might want to take a break on the grassy banks of the tarn or sheltering behind the walls of a long disused sheepfold. The onward route leaves the tarn to the east, stepping a beck and turning left (north). Descend on a stony path below Miners Crag to Castlenook Mine. From the mine retrace your steps back past the climbing hut keeping with the track to a gate to the road. Turn left to follow the road back to the parking area.

### ALONG THE WAY
**The Mines**
*For many centuries the valley of Newlands has seen its fair share of mining activity. Copper, large amounts of lead, some silver, and it is said a modicum of gold were extracted from the Goldscope Mine. The greatest period of production was in the 16th century during the reign of Elizabeth I. German miners were brought across, and production encouraged by the granting of royal patronage with the setting up, in 1561, of The Society for the Mines Royal.*

*When production declined*

*many of the mine entrances were blocked with wooden props and earth, and a tree planted as a marker. Over the years the wood has rotted and fallen into the shaft leaving the entrance open.*

**Goldscope Mine**
*The waste heaps of Goldscope overshadow Low Snab Farm. There is some suggestion that the mine was mentioned in the Class Roll of Henry III (1207-72), but it is known that German miners where working the mine in 1569. The mine opened and closed many times until 1849, when a consortium of four men bought the mine. After eighteen months, and raising about 14 tons of copper ore, all dropped out except Andrew Clark. He persevered and made his fortune by hitting the Goldscope, a very rich lead vein. The mine was abandoned in 1874.*

**Castlenook Mine**
*The mine was opened in 1860, employing four men. By 1863 a level had been driven 150 feet and the mine was producing 9 cwt of ore per fathom. A sixteen foot wheel was erected to pump out water and draw up the ore. By this time eighteen men were employed, and outside the*

dressing floors had been erected (all that remains today). It is not known when the mine closed but by this time the levels had been driven 264 feet.

### Dale Crag Mine

Sited in the crag 300 feet below the summit of Dale Head the mine was worked by Cornish miners from 1776 to 1829. It was reopened in 1833 and extensively worked for copper ore. At this time a level was driven from inside the mine, on the junction of the Borrowdale Volcanic and Skiddaw Slates, to the middle of Dale Head Crag to drain the mine of water. It is uncertain when the mine finally closed.

## KESWICK

*The name of Keswick appears to date from the 7th century, a time when the Anglian's were settling the country from the east. The generally accepted meaning for the name is "cheese farm", a combination of two Anglian elements, "cese" and "wic".*

*In 1276 the town was granted a market charter, making it an important centre for trade. But it was during the reign of Elizabeth I that Keswick was to become the centre of a major industrial complex. In 1561, Elizabeth created the Society of Mines Royal, to organise and finance the extraction of precious metals. As mining activity increased, miners were brought from Germany to improve methods and increase production.*

*Another important discovery at about the same time was that of graphite, at Seathwaite in Borrowdale. This find was to provide the raw material for what was to become Keswick's major industry, pencil manufacture.*

*During the 1800s there were at least three companies producing pencils in and around Keswick; today there is only one, and the raw materials now come from around the world.*

# WALK 7
## BRANDELHOW
## and MANESTY PARKS

*This woodland walk along the shores of Derwentwater, is one of the most pleasant walks in Lakeland. The distance craggy heights make a dramatic backdrop to the lake with sailing boats, passenger launches and the vast array of ducks and other birds who make their home along the lake shore. The return walk by a grassy terrace path contouring the slopes of Cat Bells gives splendid views over Derwentwater to Keswick overlooked by Skiddaw and Blencathra.*

**Start/Finish:** Gutherscale car park. GR246211.
**Total distance:** 8 km (5 miles).
**Height gain:** 150m (490 feet).
**Difficulty:** An easy walk through agreeable woodland, mainly on well maintained or grassy paths, wet in places with unbridged streams. A small amount of road walking.

### THE WALK

Return to the main road, cross the cattle grid and descend to a left-hand bend. Don't go round the bend, but take the path right (signposted: Hawes End, Launch Pier). At a lane turn right and follow waymarking for 200m/yds past Hawes End to an iron gate on the left. Through the gate accompany a clear track across fields to more gates. After the second gate turn left at the end of the wall to follow a path by the lakeshore to the launch pier.

Then by an on-going path along the shoreline you walk through the agreeable woodland of Brandelhow Park, linking Low and High piers. Immediately after High Brandelhow Pier bear left to keep to the shore, cross a stile and go between buildings to a gate (sign: Footpath). Continue along a driveway for 200m/yds, and opposite a cottage (The Warren) turn left on a path (signposted: Lodore).

Proceed to the shore, keep to the shoreline, cross a stile at

29

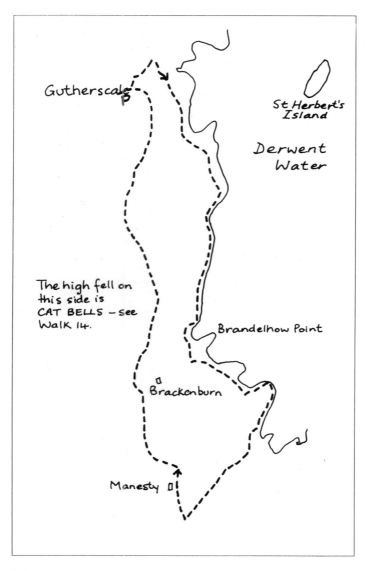

Gutherscale

St Herbert's
Island

Derwent
Water

The high fell on
this side is
CAT BELLS — see
Walk 14.

Brandelhow Point

Brackenburn

Manesty

the end of a wall, and continue on this path by the shore to wet ground at the end of the trees. Here go right, along the side of the trees to a section of boardwalks. Cross the boards then over a small mound, turn right on a grassy path, to cross the next wet area by stepping stones. Now keeping to higher dry ground make towards a wall. At the wall bear left to make for a gate at the wall corner, then by a track to the road. At the road turn right, take care with young children as the road is narrow and a popular motor route around Derwentwater.

Accompany the road for 250m/yds to pass Manesty, and take a broad track leaving the road on the left. Cross a stile, and when the path to Cat Bells leaves on the left, continue ahead round the top of the woodland to join a broad track high above the woodlands of Manesty Park and Brackenburn.

When the track meets the road continue past the quarry, and immediately take a path, left, to traverse the flanks of Cat Bells. Before meeting the road at a bend, the path passes through a stand of gorse; in spring the yellow flowers are heavily scented. At the road turn left and follow it a short distance to a junction were the lane left will return you to the car park.

## ALONG THE WAY
### Brandelhow and Manesty Parks

*Both of these properties are now in the care of the National Trust. Brandelhow Park was purchased in 1901 after an public appeal raised £6500 in only five months. Manesty was purchased shortly afterwards, in 1905. A salt well at Manesty was a popular attraction for the infirm during the 18th century.*

### Brackenburn

*Hugh Walpole (1884-1941), English novelist, stayed at Brackenburn between 1923, when he bought it, until his death. His collection of works known as "The Herries Chronicle" was set in and around Borrowdale. As you walk round the base of Cat Bells, you will find a commemorative tablet and bench erected by one of Hugh Walpole's friends.*

# WALK 8
## HIGH SPY RIDGE

*As you drive into Newlands from the north, the west face of High Spy plummets in rugged style to the wild and secluded upper reaches of Newlands valley, and belies the excellent airy walking that awaits. These rough and scarred faces rise to culminate in an outstanding ridge extending from Dalehead Tarn in the south to Swinside in the north. The complete traverse of the ridge abounds with easy walking and views.*

**Start/Finish:** Chapel Bridge, Little Town. GR221194.
**Total distance:** 10km (6miles).
**Height gain:** 640m (2099feet).
**Difficulty:** Moderate, the uphill section is on an easy gradient, and the main ridge is easy walking on a good path. The descent, however, is through a disused quarry, and young children should be kept under close control here and not allowed to enter any open mine levels.

### THE WALK
Head north-west along the road towards the hamlet of Little Town for 150m/yds to take a stile on the right. Ascend to and turn right (south) along a track, past a climbing hut to the remains of Castlenook Mine. Take a steeply climbing path, marked by a cairn, to a col near Dale Head Tarn.

Turn left (north-east) a rough path to the summit of High Spy, marked by a large cairn. The on-going route continues heading north to a shallow col. At the col leave the main path left on a grassy path near the plateau rim to a small cairn marking the summit of Maiden Moor. Keep with this path over undulating ground above Bull Crag to rejoin the main path. Descend left to Hause Gate, a grassy col connecting Cat Bells to the main ridge.

### OPTIONAL EXTRA
From Hause Gate a broad path continues north to the popular summit of Cat Bells, giving extended views over Derwent Water to Keswick and Skiddaw behind. This excursion will add

1.5km (1mile) to your day.

From the col head west (left), to a cairn. At the cairn descend left through the old mine workings on a path that is marked by small cairns. Upon meeting the valley track turn left, follow the track to a gate at the road. Turn left and follow the road a short distance to the parking area.

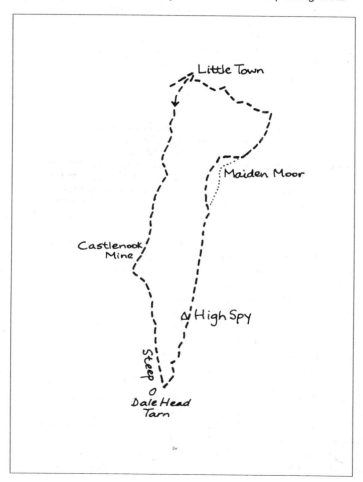

# WALK 9
## HINDSCARTH

*Viewed from Buttermere, Hindscarth looks a flat uninteresting mountain, part of a long ridge linking Dalehead with Robinson. But from the Newlands valley, Hindscarth shows itself to be one of the shapeliest fells in Lakeland, with a fine pointed summit supported by the attendant ridge of Scope End reaching far into the valley. The splendid ridge of Scope End, is narrow in places with changing views as the path switches from side to side.*

**Start/Finish:** Chapel Bridge, Little Town. GR221194.
**Total distance:** 7.5km (4½ miles).
**Height gain:** 647m (2122feet).
**Difficulty:** A walk of considerable ascent on stone and rock paths, in places exposed to steep-sided drops.

### THE WALK

Take the road across the bridge spanning Newlands Beck, to a gated lane on your left. The narrow lane leads to Newlands Chapel, and here take the left fork and gated track to Low Snab Farm. Pass through the farmyard to a gate to gain the open fellside. Ascend right to the base of the waste heaps of Goldscope Mine where a broad grass track ascends right to a fence.

Follow the fence to a clear path left, and take this path. The initial steep pull, with scrambles over rocky outcrops, soon gives way to the whole ridge to Hindscarth stretching before you. Continue along the ridge, narrow in places, the path switches from one side of the ridge to the other giving ever-changing views of the valleys below. The final steep pull to the summit passing a prominent cairn, in reality a circular shelter, which has been in view all the way. The true summit, marked by a modest cairn stands in the middle of a stony plateau a short way further on.

*For splendid views of Buttermere valley I recommend walking south to the ridge overlooking Gatesgarthdale.*

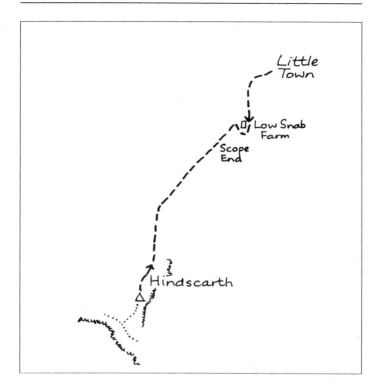

### THE WAY BACK

To return, simply retrace your steps, admiring the fine views of Newlands valley and Skiddaw en route, but taking care on the steep section of the descent.

### OPTIONAL EXTRA

In good visibility you can extend the walk by continuing south-east along the ridge — Hindscarth Edge — linking Hindscarth to the summit of Dalehead. This extra walking will add about 3.5km (2 miles) to the overall distance, but the ridge is most exhilarating.

### ALONG THE WAY
### Newlands Church and School Room

*The tiny parish church with no dedication, hiding among the trees, is well worth a visit.*

It dates mainly from 1843, when major rebuilding work was undertaken, by Reverend John Monkhouse. As for how long a church has served the valley is not known, but Saxton's map of 1576 shows a chapel on the site. Wordsworth and his daughter, while on a walking tour of the fells in May 1826, happened upon the church, which prompted a verse in his poem "To May".

Inside the church the dark oak pulpit, and reading desk communion table dating from 1610, came from Crosthwaite church, Keswick during internal refurbishment which took place in 1885. The lectern is an unusual feature with a sandstone plinth (dated 1837) and a detachable wooden top, presented to the memory of Reverend R Bott in 1937. When the top is removed the plinth is transformed into a font.

The school room was built in 1877 to replace an earlier building from 1820. With only a single class room and no more than 15 children the school was closed in 1967, but is still in regular use as a meeting room.

## KESKADALE AND BIRKRIGG OAKS

*The Keskadale and Birkrigg woodlands are comprised of oak, all Quercus petraea, and lie on steep-sided slopes at altitudes of between 1000 and 1400 feet. Unfenced and open to grazing animals, the trees are all rather small, with an average height of 17 feet. This has been attributed to the strength of the wind, since in places where trees are in shelter below crags, the height reached is much greater than those in more exposed parts of the fellsides.*

*Many of the trees have multiple trunks, but whether this is due to coppicing or fresh growth from stools after disease or burning is not known. But as most of the trees on the higher slopes have single trunks, it would seem the coppicing is the more likely explanation.*

# WALK 10
## GLENDERATERRA

*Hidden behind Skiddaw is an area virtually unknown to most visitors
to Keswick. It is a wild, intriguing place of wide, flat-bottomed,
smooth-sided valleys with broad grass and heather uplands more in
keeping with the Pennines than Lakeland. During the 19th century
this former Royal Forest was developed by the Victorians as a grouse
moor, and remained in use as such until the 1950s. This walk visits
the steep-sided valley of Glenderaterra, formerly a major lead mining
area, with the option to visit the remote row of cottages known as
Skiddaw House.*

**Start/Finish:** Latrigg car park. GR281253.
**Total distance:** 9.5km (6 miles).
**Height gain:** 340m (1115 feet).
**Difficulty:** Fairly easy, well-defined paths and farm tracks, some wet
stretches and small unbridged streams.

## THE WALK

Cross the stile at the head of the car park and turn left on a bridleway (signposted: Skiddaw, Bassenthwaite, Mosedale). Keeping the wall on your left for 350m/yds to the second gate. Through this gate bear right on a descending track into the gully of Whit Beck. Ford the beck, and follow a track across the slopes of Lonscale Fell for 1.2 km (1 mile).

To your right the view opens up of the Lake District's north/south fault, a clear division that contains the lakes of Thirlmere and Windermere along with Grasmere and Rydal Water.

At the stile, cross the fence and keep with the track as it swings left on a rock ledge into the valley of Glenderaterra. The onward route now follows a high level route for 1.5 km (11/4 miles) to cross a beck by a wooden bridge. Proceed for 100m/yds to the path junction near a stone wall, marked by a guide stone.

## OPTIONAL EXTRA

From here it is possible to visit the remote youth hostel at

Skiddaw House. For almost half a century the shepherd, Pearson Dalton, lived here alone with his dogs and a cat for company. Surrounded by the only substantial stand of trees in the area, Skiddaw House, until 1971 must have been the loneliest shepherd's house in England.

Heading north from the junction keep the wall to your right for 500m/yds. Leaving the wall behind strike out across the fell side on a clear grassy path to gate and stone wall. Through the gate follow the path northwest to a bridge spanning Salehow Beck, and take a rising path to a group of pine trees sheltering Skiddaw House. Return by the same route.

This extension to one of the most remote houses in England will add 3km (2 miles) to your day.

### THE WAY BACK

Turn right, now with a wall on your left for 400m/yds make for a ladder stile. Cross the stile, then two wooden footbridges, and in a short distance arrive at a traditional slate bridge, spanning Roughton Gill.

Cross the bridge to gain a good vehicle track which is followed to a car park at the mouth of the glen. Make for the cattle grid at the car park entrance, but don't cross it. Instead take the (signposted) gated path on the right and descend to the buildings of Blencathra Centre. At a main track turn right (signpost: Keswick) between the buildings to a signpost directing you right (Derwent Fold and Keswick). Now waymarkings take you left across a field and along the edge of a pine plantation, to a stile at a lane.

Turn right and along the lane to a visible group of buildings (Derwent Fold). At the first building turn left on a gated track (signposted) to a wooden bridge spanning Glenderaterra Beck. Cross the bridge and take a rising path to a rough vehicle track. Turn right and ascend for 200m/yds and then turn left. In a few strides turn right on a track (signposted: Skiddaw, Underscar) which climbs among grouse bushes to a pine plantation. Keeping the plantation to your right go through two gate, then on a clear track make north west for 400m/yds returning to Latrigg car park.

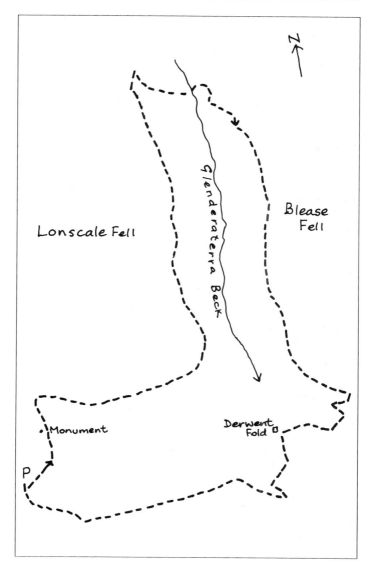

# WALK 11
## BARROW AND STONYCROFT GILL

*Barrow, with its fine cone shape and long grassy ridge, makes an excellent mountain on which to introduce younger members of the family to the pleasures of mountain walking. Situated at the mouth of Newlands and Coledale valleys, this modest fell offers unspoiled views of the Causey Pike ridge to the south, and the grand summit of Grisedale Pike to the north.*

**Start/Finish:** Parking area above Farm Uzzicar, GR233217.
**Total distance:** 9.5km (6 miles).
**Height gain:** 330m (1082feet).
**Difficulty:** None, apart from an ascent on grassy paths; a rough mountain track is used for the descent.

### THE WALK
Head north along the road towards Keswick for 600m/yds, and then go left on a bridleway to climb above a pine plantation and continue a short distance to a signposted junction above Braithwaite Lodge.

Turn left to begin a steady upward plod from the junction to a minor summit. The way ahead lies across a shallow col, to the right and left of which can be seen evidence of 18th century lead mining. Continue on a narrow grassy ridge, finally arriving at a small cairn marking the summit of Barrow.

The summit views extend east over Derwent Water to Helvel-lyn, while to the north the ruggedness of Blencathra, Skiddaw and Barf, contrast with the flat waters of Bassenthwaite Lake. To the south Stonycroft Gill (our return route) is contained by the steep grassy slops of the Causey Pike ridge.

### THE WAY BACK
You could simply retrace your steps, a prospect enhanced by the fine views across Derwent Water. But take care, the grass when wet can be very slippery. A better alternative is to follow the on-going path (west) down to meet a crosspath at the col with Stile End. At the col turn left, and use a contouring path

40

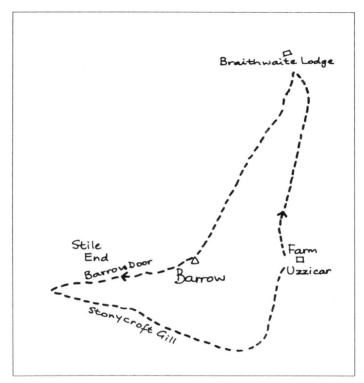

to meet a track beside Stonycroft Gill. Turn left, on the track to descend alongside the gill with its many cascades and mining remains. Now simply follow the track back to the parking area.

## ALONG THE WAY
### Barrow Mines

*Extensive mining took place on the slopes of Barrow. The main site was on the slopes above Uzzicar Farm. As you a return by Stonycroft Gill, just above the bridge, are the remains of a drainage channel that diverted water from a dam higher upstream. Directly below the dam a mine shaft had been made deep into the stream bed. Some years ago, the dam burst and the water, reverting to its original course, poured into the mine, with considerable loss of life.*

# WALK 12
## SKIDDAW

*Skiddaw was at one time considered to be one of the most intimidating mountain climbs in Lakeland. The Victorians would use the services of a guide and a pony for the ascent; resting at the Half Way House for refreshments. This walk leaves the popular tourist track used by the Victorians, and those who climb Skiddaw today, for the seclusion of Whit Beck and Jenkin Hill.*

**Start/Finish:** Latrigg car park, Gale Road, Applethwaite. GR281253.
**Total distance:** 10km (6 miles).
**Height gain:** 750m (2460feet).
**Difficulty:** Demanding, with considerable height gain over a distance of 5km (3 miles). Plentiful words of encouragement, praise and good supply of stops to admire the view will ensure any child making this standard of ascent for the first time does not become dispirited. Not to be under taken in poor weather.

### THE WALK

The walk begins by crossing the stile at the head of the car park, then left alongside a wall, (signposted; Skiddaw, Bassenthwaite, Mosedale).

Proceed through two gates and follow the path past a small monument to the memory of the Hawell family, shepherds noted for their skill as breeders of Herdwick sheep on Lonscale Fell. Keep with the path as it climbs to a gate and two stiles.The flat ground to your right is the site of the long gone Half Way House, and is still an ideal spot to stop and admire the view back over Keswick and Derwent Water.

Over the stile continue for 250m/yds to a wall corner, and there turn right on a grassy path alongside wall/fence. At the end of the wall bear left on a path leading to a small iron gate on the col. Don't go through the gate, but turn left and follow the fence passing the summit cairn of Jenkin Hill on the way to the main path at a gate.

The raising path ahead makes for the summit of Little Man, but we shall leave this for the return journey when it requires less climbing.

Go through the gate, then on a broad path (with splendid views of Blencathra and Mosedale), to a second gate. From here it is a short journey northwards, rocky in places to the trig and stone shelters on the summit of Skiddaw.

## THE WAY BACK

Suitably rested and having identified the distant views, with the help of the nearby indicator,

erected in 1977 to mark the Silver Jubilee of Elizabeth II, the return starts by retracing your steps over Skiddaw's south summit to the gate.

Don't go through the gate but make right, then left, following the fence to the top of Little Man. From the top Little Man descend alongside the fence to join the main path. Turn right, follow the path to the gate at the Half Way House. From here retrace your steps to the car park.

# WALK 13
## SWINSIDE

*A pleasant walk along country lanes, across open fields and along the banks of Newlands Beck, where you will discover the remains of old hedge growth. The return is a woodland walk to the shore of Derwent Water before heading back to Portinscale.*

**Start/Finish:** Suspension bridge Portinscale. GR253237.
**Total distance:** 8km (5miles).
**Height gain:** 120m (394feet).
**Difficulty:** Fairly easy, presenting no problems of route finding or ascent. Care will be needed with young children when alongside Newlands Beck.

## THE WALK

From the parking area cross the suspension bridge, and continue past the hotels to a road junction. Turn right for 200m/yds, passing Dorothy's Well to a footpath on left (signposted: Ullock). Take this path, first a lane between houses, then a path to a gate. Here cross a lane, left, to a path between beech hedges.

Cross a small bridge, then follow field paths to the road at Ullock. Turn right on the narrow road, past farm buildings, for 1km/½ mile to a junction. Here turn right and accompany the road for 200m/yds to the bridge spanning Newlands Beck. Just

before the bridge take the gated footpath on the left, keep on this path for 1.1 km/½ mile, crossing two stiles, until you reach a stone packhorse bridge spanning the beck.

Cross the bridge and use a fenced track to Farm Uzzicar. Go through the farmyard to the entrance gate. Through the gate turn left on a grassy track to a stile at the fence corner. Continue, first with a fence on your left, then an old hedge, to cross a fence. Follow the fence left (waymarked) a short distance and bear right on a track beside Newlands Beck to the road at Stair.

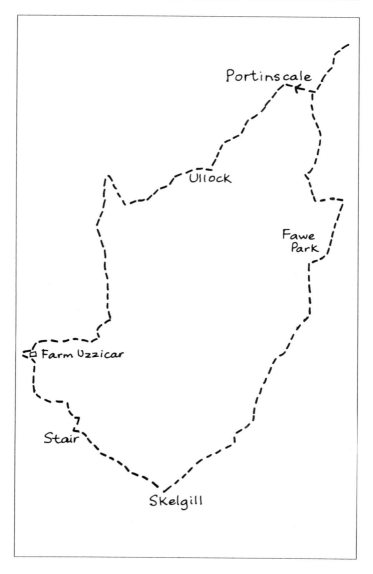

## TO CONTINUE

Make left over the bridge and at the cross roads continue ahead on gated road (signposted: Skelgill). Now use this narrow lane for half a mile to Skelgill. Pass between the farm buildings. Go through the gate and use the lane below Cat Bells for 500m/yds to the main road.

Keep left, cross the cattle grid, and as road bends left take a signposted footpath on the right. Descend to a lane, take a gated footpath (signposted: Portinscale, Keswick) between fenced woodland to cross the driveway of Lingholm, and on past Fawe Park to Nichol End Marina. On reaching the marina turn left along the lane to the road, then turn right along the road for half a mile. Where the road bends left, go right down past hotels to retrace your steps over the suspension bridge.

## ALONG THE WAY
**Portinscale Bridge**

*A twin arch bridge used to span the River Derwent carrying the main road linking Keswick with the village of Portinscale. In 1907 the highway authority condemned the bridge, a campaign by Canon Rawnsley resulted in major repair work taking place in 1913 and a engineer of the time pronounced it "only vulnerable to dynamite". Alas, it was not dynamite, but a heavy flood during December 1954 which caused damaged beyond repair to the bridge. A temporary Callander Hamilton steel bridge replaced the fine old stone bridge, this remained in use until the new A66 road bypassed Portinscale at which time the present suspension bridge was erected.*

## CENTURY THEATRE, KESWICK

*Until November 1996, occupying a site in a corner of the car park near the boat landing stages in Keswick, four large trailers were affectionately known as the "Blue Box Theatre". The trailers were built in 1952 at Hinckley in Leicestershire as one of the country's first travelling theatres. Since the 1960s, the theatre has remained in Keswick, playing to full houses for many seasons. A new building is to replace the trailers, which are now at a museum 8 miles from where they were built.*

# WALK 14
## CAT BELLS RIDGE

*Cat Bells being within easy reach of Keswick will for many be their first taste of fell walking. If you choose a summer evening or early morning start, the views will be forever changing as you gain height and as the light changes. Most walkers climb and descend Cat Bells by the same route, but by crossing the summit and descending into Yewthwaite Gill a more interesting walk is possible.*

**Start/Finish:** Gutherscale Car Park, GR246211.
**Total distance:** 4.5km (3 miles).
**Height gain:** 349m (1145feet).
**Difficulty:** A fairly energetic walk, but otherwise undemanding, on good paths. Young children will need restraining on the descent near Yewthwaite Gill and must not be allowed to enter any open mine levels.

### THE WALK

On a paved path, leave the car park and head back towards the road, passing a path on left. Avoid any tempting shortcuts, as a twisting path makes a steady pull to a rock outcrop. The outcrop can be easily passed on the left, although the more adventurous may scramble a small central gully marked by a plaque to "Thomas Arthur Leonard."

Above the outcrop stay with the path to the minor of summit, Brandlehow, from where the summit of Cat Bells is clearly seen ahead. Then follow a well trodden path along a delightful ridge, to a short pull that brings you to Cat Bells' rocky summit dome.

*The views are astounding in all directions: looking west are the splendid fells of Coledale, Eel Crag, Sail and Grisedale Pike. To the north Keswick and Bassenthwaite Lake are overshadowed by the grey slopes of Skiddaw. Further right, you see the distinctive profile of Blencathra.*

*A well earned break can be enjoyed in one of the numerous spots in which to seclude oneself around the summit.*

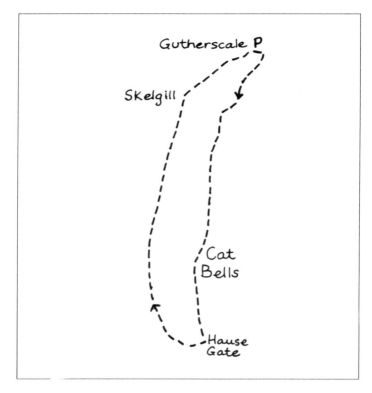

## THE WAY BACK

When suitably recovered (other than retracing one's steps) the way back lies in continuing across the top of Cat Bells on a wide path down to Hause Gate, the broad grassy col between Cat Bells and Maiden Moor to the south.

At the col, turn right (west), to a large cairn and a fork in the path. Here you have a splendid view into Yewthwaite Gill and Newlands valley. Keep to the right-hand, upper path above quarry remains. Passing an almost hidden adit, the path turns right and descends to meet a wall. With the wall to your left, accompany it for 800m/yds to meet a tarmac lane at Skelgill. Now simply follow the lane the short distance to the car park.

## ALONG THE WAY
### Cat Bells

*Cat Bells takes its name almost certainly from the wild cat, that roamed many of the English Forest until the 18th century. Though still present in small numbers in remote parts of Scotland, the last wild cat in England was killed in Northumberland in 1853. In old English "Cat" would have been "Catt", while "Bells" originates from the Middle English word "belde", to give a combined meaning of "the den of the wild cat".*

### St Herbert's Island

*From the ridge of Cat Bells there is a prominent view of St Herbert's Island on Derwent Water. According to the Venerable Bede, St Herbert was a friend of the better known St Cuthbert and chose the island for his hermitage "to avoid the intercourse of man, and that nothing might withdraw his attention from unceasing mortification and prayer". Each year Herbert met Cuthbert in Carlisle, but in 687, Cuthbert, having a presentiment of his death, told Herbert that he would not see him again. "When Herbert heard this he fell down at his feet, and with many sighs and tears beseeched him, for the love of the Lord, that he would not forsake him, but remember his faithful brother and associate, and make intercession with the gracious God, that they might depart hence into heaven together." The request seems to have been heeded since both men died on the 19th of March 687.*

---

### LAKELAND PHOTOGRAPHERS

*The Lake District was a favoured location for many of the early photographers, attracted there not only by the scenery, but by the high numbers of tourists. while many photographers preferred to use a studio, there were a few notable pioneers who were prepared to venture into the outdoors. Among these, the Abraham brothers, and the pioneering rock climber O.G. Jones, produced many remarkable pictures.*

# WALK 15
## CAUSEY PIKE

*In later years, the Braithwaite Horseshoe, extended beyond Causey Pike to encompass Grisedale Pike will make a fine energetic day out on the hills. But for now this magnificent walk, including its sensational final pull to the rocky summit of Causey Pike, will be quite enough for young legs. Followed by a fine walk on the grassy plateau of Scar Crags with dramatic views down the crags into Rigg Beck, the walk makes is a splendid introduction to the pleasures of mountain ridge walking for the young and not so young alike.*

**Start/Finish:** Parking area, Uzzicar Farm. GR233217.
**Total distance:** 7.5 km (4½ miles).
**Height gain:** 592m (1942feet).
**Difficulty:** A sustained mountain walk, with 2km (1¼ miles) of continuous, steady ascent.

### THE WALK

From the parking area head left along the road (500m/yds) to cross a small stone bridge spanning Stonycroft Gill. A short distance after the bridge take a signposted footpath on the right. Pass a wooden seat and continue to climb, ignoring any paths which may seem easier options.

The path climbs steeply to the top of Rowling End, marked by a small cairn. After a break to recover your breath, the way continues by the clear path heading west along the ridge to a shallow col. The rocky cone of Causey Pike, appears, towering above. After a short uphill walk, the final rocky pull to the summit will delight most children, though it will require the use of hands near the top.

### THE WAY BACK

Once the summit is reached, a rocky dome marked with a small cairn, take time to reward your efforts with the fine all round mountain panorama.

Leave the summit on a rocky path, to gain the ridge running south of west, along which there

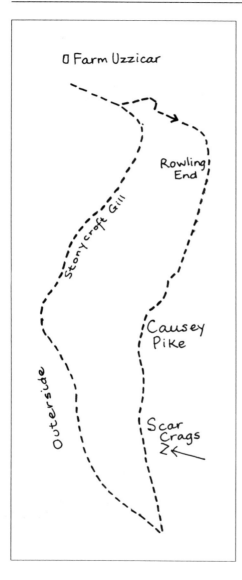

are many places to shelter should you require a longer break. The way, is now by a grassy path marked by cairns, to the next fell, Scar Crags. Higher than Causey Pike, the flat summit of Scar Crags is marked by a large cairn to the right of the path, which keeps close to the edge of the crag, giving spectacular views into Rigg Beck below. Cross the grassy plateau, south-west, then descend to the col below Sail.

At the col turn right (north-east) on an initially indistinct path across scree, but which soon joins a broad track. The track is now followed and descends on the left bank of Stonycroft Gill, below Outerside and Barrow to meet the road opposite the parking area.

# WALK 16
## OUTERSIDE

*Outerside tends to be neglected in favour of many of the higher fells which surround it. This neglect usually means that you get the day to yourself, a delightful day spent on grassy paths with spectacular views of the surrounding fells.*

**Start/Finish:** Braithwaite Church, GR229236.
**Total distance:** 7km (4½ miles).
**Height gain:** 515m (1690feet).
**Difficulty:** Moderate, on good farm tracks and grassy paths, care will be needed on the grassy descents.

### THE WALK

As there is only limited parking near Braithwaite church, it is better to use the small car park at the end of the track to Force Crag Mine on the B5292, opposite the Hope Memorial Camp. From the car park walk back down the road towards the village, and cross the bridge spanning Coledale Beck. Across the bridge turn right and in a short distance arrive at the church.

From the church take the road past the Coledale Inn. Keep with the tarmac lane for 400m/yds as it bends right and climbs to a gated farm track. Over the stile keep with the track to the ruined buildings of High Coledale. As the track swings right into the

farm, continue ahead on a wide grassy trod to meet an eroded path into Barrow Door, the col between Barrow and Stile End. When you arrive at this eroded path take the grassy path ascending right.

A short steady pull soon brings you to on the summit of Stile End, marked by a small cairn, with views of Skiddaw and Blencathra to the north and the Helvellyn range to the east.

Leave Stile End for the boggy col of Low Moss. At the col make left then right, around a small tarn, to gain a clear zigzagging path to the summit of Outerside. The top flattens as you approach the modest cairn marking the highest point.

Enclosed by higher fells Outerside has restricted views into the head of Coledale, though the Causey Pike ridge and broken crags of Eel Crag to the left are impressive enough. To the right, across the deep recess of Coledale, is the high coned shape of Grisedale Pike, with the workings of Force Crag mine in the valley below.

## TO CONTINUE

From the top of Outerside descend westerly on a grass path to join a stone track. Turn left and follow the track to a cairn marking a path on the left. Take this path to the col of Barrow Door, and, now with Barrow Gill on your right, descend to rejoin the track at High Coledale Farm, from where you can easily retrace your steps to Braithwaite.

## ALONG THE WAY
### Force Crag Mine

*It is possible that there were workings on or around the site of the mine during the reign of Elizabeth I. A report by 7th Earl of Northumberland, Thomas Percy, stated: "The crust ore at Coledale holds 125 tunne of Lead which holdeth 15oz of Silver per tunne".*

*Major exploration dose not*

*appear to have taken place until during the early 1800s when a lease was taken out to work for lead. Over the years the mine has been worked by a number of companies, all working to extract the many minerals including lead, zinc and barytes. The mine was worked until 1992 when, following a market fall in the price of barytes, the mine finally closed.*

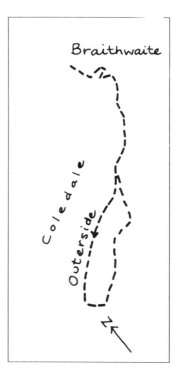

# WALK 17
## CASTLERIGG STONE CIRCLE

*The most common approach to Castlerigg Stone Circle is by car on a narrow lane from Keswick. By contrast this varied walk takes you first by a lakeshore, then ascends through mixed woodland. to fields and lanes enclosed by stone walls. The scenery is of the highest order throughout, with fine views of Derwent Water, Bassenthwaite Lake and the surrounding fells.*

**Start/Finish:** Car park, near NT information centre, at Keswick boatlandings.
**Total distance:** 11.5km (7 miles).
**Height gain:** 170m (558 feet).
**Difficulty:** Moderate, on well maintained paths and forestry tracks, but care should be taken as this walk crosses three major roads.

### THE WALK

Leave the car park and turn left to walk past the launch piers towards Friar's Crag. Shortly after the road end take the path left along the lakeshore to enter a small woodland, keep with the path as it bends right to a gated track.

Turn left, cross a cattle grid and head towards the road. Before reaching the road turn right on a path, marked by a boundary stone (R.D.M. 1831), continue through the trees, then between a wall and fence.

At the end of the fence look for a gap in the wall on your right. Through the gap, turn left along the road for 50m/yds to a gated track on the right (signposted).

Keep with the track as it climbs through Great Wood for 1.3 km (1 mile), and bends right to a path on the left (signposted: Rakefoot, Walla Crag). Here make back left, for 300m/yds to a path junction, above Brockle Beck.

Turn right (signposted: Castlerigg Stone Circle, Walla Crag). Keep the beck on your left for 250m/yds then cross it at a bridge, and make for the gate across the field, leading to a lane. Through the gate go left for 10m/yds to a signposted path

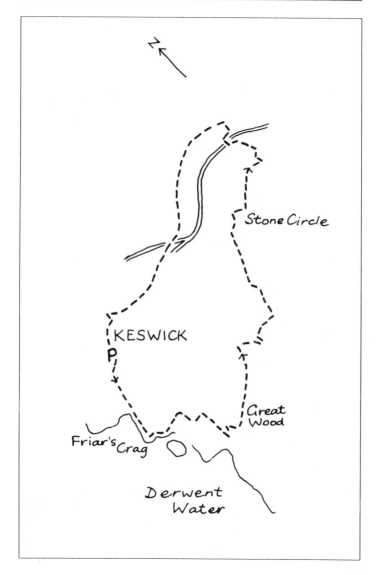

on your right. Take this path and keep the wall to your left. Cross a ladder stile, turn left to cross another stile, then, keeping a fence on your left, continue to a gate at a main road (A591).

Cross the road, then continue ahead an a narrow lane for 1 km (3/4 mile), and look for a stone barn in a field on the right, shortly after which take a stile over the wall into a field containing Castlerigg Stone Circle.

## THE WAY BACK

Leave the stone circle in a northerly direction, heading for a gate and the road. Though the gate turn right and keep with the road past Goosewell Farm to a road junction. Turn left, and left again at the next junction. Continue along this road for 300m/yds to a left bend, at the far end of the crash barrier go right, down steps to cross the A66 road.

Across the road, turn right and then left over a stile, then descend to meet the old Keswick railway track. Turn left and keep with the track as it accompanies the River Greta to Keswick Station. From the station platform go left between the station buildings and the swimming pool, from where it is a simple matter to make your way across town to the car park.

## ALONG THE WAY
### Castlerigg Stone Circle

*Dating from 3000-2500 BC, the Neolithic structure predates Stonehenge by over a thousand years. The outer circle of 38 stones is more of an oval and measures 30.5m (100ft) at its widest point, while to the eastern side is a rectangle of 10 stones. Excavations during the last century found only charcoal remains in the rectangle and three stone axes in th main circle.*

*A curious fact is that a line drawn north to south across the two highest stones connects the summits of Skiddaw and Helvellyn. John Keats recounted his visit to the circle in 1818 in the poem "Hyperion" with the lines:*

> *"like a dismal cirque*
> *Of Druid stones upon a*
> *forlorn moor,*
> *When the chill rain begins*
> *at shut of eve".*

# WALK 18
## BRUNDHOLME WOOD

*When I first came to Keswick as a child, steam trains still plied the line
between Penrith and Cockermouth. I didn't know then where Penrith
or Cockermouth were; all that mattered was to stand on the platform
and watch the splendid old trains steam into the station and disgorge
passengers from distant places. Now forty years on, the trains have
gone and the sidings have been turned into a car park. But the trackbed
is still there, and has been made into a footpath and cycle way, using
the old bridges to cross the River Greta many times as it passes
through a beautiful wooded gorge.*

**Start/Finish:** Platform of the disused railway station behind Keswick
Spar. GR272238.
**Total distance:** 5.5km (3½ miles).
**Height gain:** 150m (490 feet).
**Difficulty:** An easy walk, mainly on the old railway path and good
woodland trails.

### THE WALK
Leave the station platform and
head east towards Penrith on
the old railway track, soon crossing the River Greta. Keep with
the railway as it passes under
an arched road bridge, to a set
of double gates under the A66
flyover. Go through the gates,
turn right and climb to meet the
road. On meeting the road descend immediately left to rejoin
the railway above a weir.

Now keep with the railway
until you arrive at the third bridge
across the River Greta.

Over the bridge take the stiled
path left (signposted: Keswick
via Brundholme Wood). Cross
the field to the next stile into
Brundholme Wood; cross the
stile and descend to the river.
Now follow the river downstream to a set of steps, continue ahead up the steps to a
crosspath. At the next junction
turn left (signposted: Keswick).
Keep with this path as it climbs
and falls to meet the river at a
number of points until you go
under the flyover again.

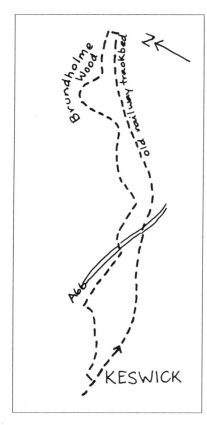

300m/yds to a sign directing you left for Keswick. Turn left into the drive for Brundholme Country House for 10m/yds, then turn right on a waymarked path to Keswick. Keep with the path as it passes the back of Keswick Bridge Time Share to the road. Turn left towards the bridge, then climb the steps to rejoin the railway. Turn right, and the station is ahead of you.

### ALONG THE WAY
### Brigham

*During the heyday of the Mines Royal Company in the reign of Elizabeth I, a large smelting mill and forge were built at Brigham. A weir was built across the Greta and a mill race supplied a source of power to the smelting works.*

*In the late 1800s Keswick became an early pioneer in the use of hydroelectric power when a generating plant was built at Brigham Forge. Using power from the weir and mill race the generators provided power until 1940s when the Central Electricity Generating Board took over responsibility for the supply.*

Shortly after the flyover you arrive at the village of Brigham. Don't go through the gate, but go right, up steps, to accompany the path through the trees to join a road at the riding stables for The Calvert Trust.

Go left along the road for

# WALK 19
## SWINSIDE FROM LITTLE TOWN

*A few years ago I was planning a walk across Scotland with a lot of 3000-ft summits in it. A friend said to me: "You know, Ron, not all the pleasures in Scotland are above 3000 feet". How right he was; I had a wonderful two weeks walking enjoying the straths and glens.*
*The same can be said for the Lake District; the valleys hold many treasures which are lost to walkers bound for the high tops. With wild flowers in abundance, birds in the hedgerows, fish in Newlands Beck, there is a lot be said for a valley walk.*

**Start/Finish:** Chapel Bridge, Little Town. GR232194.
**Total distance:** 8.5km (5 miles).
**Height gain:** 300m (984 feet).
**Difficulty:** An easy walk on tracks and field paths.
Care will be needed on narrow roads.

### THE WALK

From Chapel Bridge start by making your way along the road for 300m/yds to Little Town. Continue through the village to a farm track on the right (signposted: Skelgill). Turn right along the track, and at a junction go left through a gate. Keep with the track as it crosses Yewthwaite Gill until you arrive at a cottage.

From the cottage take a track heading north-east to a gate, and through the gate keep with the track, first with a hedge to your left and later on your right to the farm buildings at Skelgill.

Go through the farm buildings to the road, turn right to a gate, and through the gate continue ahead on a narrow lane for 500m/yds to the main road at Gutherscale.

On meeting the main road bear left to cross a cattle grid as the road descends. Keep with the road for 0.75km (½ mile) to a road to the left (signposted: Stair ¾ mile). Turn left and continue past Swinside Inn, and about 100m/yds past the inn look for a signposted footpath to the right. Take the path across fields until you meet Newlands Beck, Now follow the beck

59

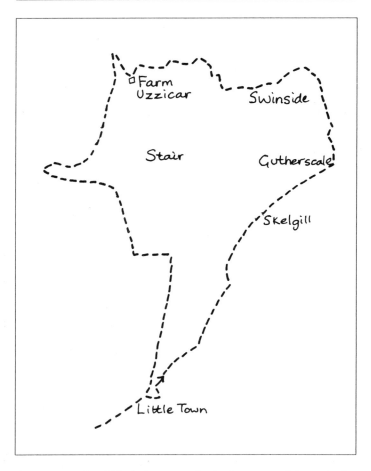

downstream for 150m/yds to a stone bridge.

Cross the bridge and go through the gate to an enclosed track. Now accompany the track for 500m/yds to Uzzicar Farm.

At the farm turn right and take the farm access road to the main road. Go left along the road for 200m/yds to a track (signposted: Footpath) ascending to your right. Take the track for 0.75km (½ mile) to the remains of a mine waste heap.

Now look for and take a track descending left to Stonycroft Gill.

Cross the beck by stepping stones and follow a broad grassy trod ascending back left. Keep with this path until you meet the road near Rowling End Farm. At the road go right, past the farm for 100m/yds, and then look for and take a gated footpath on the left (signposted: Ghyll Bank).

First enclosed by trees, the path crosses the access to Rowling End Farm, then by field paths and a bridge spanning Newlands Beck to a road at Ghyll Bank. At the road turn right; it is now an easy matter of following the road for 1 km (¾ mile) to Little Town, and then retracing your steps to Chapel Bridge.

## NEWLANDS VALLEY

*Outside the higher parts of Lakeland valleys, peasant colonisation was the main factor in developing the framework of settlements. The 12th and 13th centuries were a time of steady population expansion, and almost every county contained farms and hamlets whose lands were taken from the wilderness area around. The Newlands valley was one such area, and estate records show the taking-in of fields from the rugged fellsides between 1266 and 1310.*
*The valley also saw many lead mines developed during the mid to late 19th century in response to town and city demands for lead piping, water tanks and roofing materials.*

# WALK 20
## KNOTT RIGG
## from Rigg Beck

*Knott Rigg and Ard Crags offer an outstanding ridge walk that is neglected by many walkers favouring the greater heights; as a result, here lies an opportunity to get away from the crowds.*
*The splendid views of the higher fells, and into Buttermere will more than reward the initial steep ascent, and words of encouragement to young children will ensure a rewarding and enjoyable day is experienced by everyone.*
*The summit of Knott Rigg is confusing in poor visibility, and counsels against tackling this walk in these conditions.*

**Start/Finish:** Disused quarry, near the bridge spanning Rigg Beck. GR229201.
**Total distance:** 8km (5 miles).
**Height gain:** 571m (1873 feet).
**Difficulty:** A fine grassy ridge walk; unbridged rigg Beck needs to be crossed near the start of the walk. The descent to Keskadale Farm is steep, and can be slippery when wet.

### THE WALK

A small wooden signpost near the bridge directs you uphill alongside Rigg Beck, on a broad path. Keep with the path, first beside the stream, and then by a stone wall. At the end of the wall, turn left to cross Rigg Beck by stepping stones, followed by a short pull alongside a fence and wall to a wall corner.

The way is now to the right, on a path through bracken, to an obvious path which clam- bers energetically to the ridge above. Once the initial steepness is overcome, the onward walk to the first summit, Ard Crags, is quite easy.

The grassy top of Ard Crags, marked by a small cairn, from which you can see the ridge running on to Knott Rigg, set against the backdrop of Robinson, Red Pike and Whiteless Pike.

Leave the summit on a grassy ridge to a shallow col, with fine views down Ill Gill (on the left) to the Newlands valley. Ascend the grassy slope beyond to reach the large grassy summit of Knott rigg, marked by a small cairn on a slate outcrop.

## THE WAY BACK

Leave the summit in an easterly direction and head 200m/yds towards two small ponds enclosed by fences. Pass between the ponds to gain a path on an undulating ridge above Ill Gill. Descend on a grassy path, first through heather, then bracken, changing direction to avoid rocky outcrops, to a wall. Take great care as you descend, especially after rain.

At the wall, go left. Keep with the wall past farm buildings (Keskadale Farm) to reach the road. Turn left and descends bends to a gated footpath (signposted) on the right. Take this path and keep the stream to your right. When the path crosses the stream go through a gate, and turn left to a bridge spanning Keskadale Beck. Cross the bridge, and keeping the beck to your left, make for an obvious track climbing to the remains of a stone wall.

From the wall, head towards a stile near a large oak tree at the end of a row of trees. Over the stile, continue with a fence

to the right for 300m/yds to the third stile. Cross the stile and follow the marker posts across marshy ground dotted with hawthorns to reach a stile at the end of a wall. Continue across the next two fields to the road to Low High Snab.

At the road, turn left, passing Newlands church to a gate. Through the gate, turn left, and follow the road to the junction at a purple house. Turn right and you will return to the bridge spanning Rigg Beck from where you started.

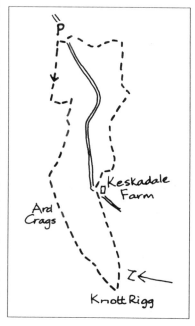

# QUESTA
## Walks with Children

are intended to encourage young (and the not-so-young, any more) to get out into our countryside.

All the guidebooks are written by experienced authors, all of whom are members of the Outdoor Writers' Guild, a national organisation of writers and photographers, painters, designers, editors and publishers, dedicated to the pursuit and enjoyment of informal recreation in our natural countryside.

The walks in this series of books are meant to serve as a genuine introduction to countryside walking, and in this respect they are equally suitable for parents who may be coming to walking for the first time.

All the walks have been walked and checked by the author(s) during the compilation of the guidebooks.

Titles (and forthcoming titles) in the series are:

Walks with Children in the Lake District:
*Buttermere and the Vale of Lorton*
*Borrowdale*
*Patterdale*
*Around Coniston*
*Ambleside and Grasmere*
*Around Kendal* (1999)

Walks with Children in the Surrey Hills

Walks with Children in the Yorkshire Dales:
*Swaledale and Wensleydale*
*Wharfedale*
*Around Malham and Ribblesdale* (1999)